BRIGH

THE CATCHER IN THE RYE BY J.D. SALINGER

Intelligent Education

INFLUENCE PUBLISHERS

Nashville, Tennessee

BRIGHT NOTES: The Catcher in the Rye

www.BrightNotes.com

No part of this publication may be used or reproduced in any manner whatsoever without written permission, except in the case of brief quotations in critical articles and reviews. For permissions, contact Influence Publishers http://www.influencepublishers.com.

ISBN: 978-1-645422-60-0 (Paperback)
ISBN: 978-1-645422-61-7 (eBook)

Published in accordance with the U.S. Copyright Office Orphan Works and Mass Digitization report of the register of copyrights, June 2015.

Originally published by Monarch Press.
Charlotte A. Alexander; Francis X. Sauer; John Hurley; W. John Campbell; Laurie Rozakis, 1965
2019 Edition published by Influence Publishers.

Interior design by Lapiz Digital Services. Cover Design by Thinkpen Designs.

Printed in the United States of America.

Library of Congress Cataloging-in-Publication Data forthcoming.
Names: Intelligent Education
Title: BRIGHT NOTES: The Catcher in the Rye
Subject: STU004000 STUDY AIDS / Book Notes

CONTENTS

INTRODUCTION TO J. D. SALINGER

J. D. Salinger (Jerome David Salinger) was born in New York City in 1919 to Sol and Miriam Jillich Salinger (his father was Jewish; his mother, Scotch Irish). He has a sister Doris 8 years his senior. He attended public schools on Manhattan's upper West Side, the private McBurney School in Manhattan, and then Valley Forge Military Academy in Pennsylvania, from which he graduated in 1936. His college experience was brief: a summer session at New York University, a short-story writing class at Columbia University taught by Whit Burnett, co-editor of *Story*, and a short period at Ursinus College in Pennsylvania.

Uninterested in joining his father's meat importing business, he was writing fiction at least by the time he was twenty (his first published story is dated 1940). Of further biographical note is his military service during World War II, including counter-intelligence training in Devonshire, England (the setting for part of *"For Esme-with Love and Squalor"*); he also participated in D-Day beach landings and European campaigns. During the post-war period he has lived, in addition to New York, in Tarry-town, N.Y.; Westport, Conn. and Cornish, N.H.

In 1955 he married Claire Douglas; they have a daughter and a son.

Salinger is noted for what has been called a "reverse exhibitionism," that is, a determination to keep his life private. If he is a recluse, however it seems to have become so by a more gradual process than is usually pointed out (he was, after all, in this teen years, an active student at Valley Forge prep school, participating in several clubs, the dramatic organization, and in the preparation of the academy yearbook as literary editor). Withdrawal may have been the result of disenchantment perhaps with the irritant, nuisance element success can bring, as well as a general seeking after a peaceful existence which was not uncommon to young men who survived the grim years of actual involvement in World War II. In 1950, for example, he was not above visiting (while living at Tarrytown, N. Y.) a short-story class at Sarah Lawrence College, although he remarked afterward, "I enjoyed the day, but it isn't something I'd ever want to do again." Since then he has turned down invitations for public appearances (such as participation in the various writers' conferences which are run regularly in the United States and abroad).

In Cornish, N. H., where he has lived since the fervor of publicity over *The Catcher in the Rye*, he seems to have stressed in "nuisance values" of success, by putting a high fence around his house. Since this is the case, it seems a wise policy to follow the lead of one of Salinger's more scrupulous critics (Warren French) who admits in the preface to his book about the author (J. D. Salinger): "I bear no news about Salinger himself-I would consider it impertinent to invade his cherished privacy."

BACKGROUND AND PUBLICATION OF *NINE STORIES*

By 1941, when he was 22, Salinger was publishing in well-paying magazines such as *Collier's and Esquire*, and he continued to write during World War II. But it was in 1948 that he began to find real recognition, with the publication of three stories which later were to appear in the collection, *Nine Stories:* *"A Perfect Day for Bananafish," "Uncle Wiggily in Connecticut,"* and *"Just Before the War with the Eskimos,"* all appearing in the *New Yorker*, certainly a prestigious sign. In 1949 and 1950 three more stories from his collection were published - *"The Laughing Man," "Down at the Dinghy,"* and *"For Esme - with Love and Squalor."* The collection itself, of course, was not issued until 1953, since when it has enjoyed lasting popularity without ever reaching the top-selling levels. (The story *"Uncle Wiggily in Connecticut,"* titled *My Foolish Heart*, was turned into a movie by Samuel Goldwyn studios with Susan Hayward and Dana Andrews. It was a distorted version which Salinger disapproved of highly, a factor which has probably contributed to urge his continuing refusal to allow further screen or television productions of his writings.)

BACKGROUND AND PUBLICATION OF *CATCHER IN THE RYE*

In the late '40s and early '50s, while the pieces from *Nine Stories* were being published separately, Salinger was undoubtedly trying to work into a novel his earlier stories about Holden Caulfield. (In 1946, for instance, a novelette about Holden had been accepted for publication, then was withdrawn by Salinger). *The Catcher in the Rye* became upon publication in 1951 what might be termed an almost-immediate success. As a midsummer Book-of-the-Month Club selection, for example, it certainly exposed Salinger to a larger audience than he had hitherto enjoyed-if, indeed, "enjoyed" is the proper word, since the degree of popularity was enough to disturb Salinger, who directed that a large photograph of his face be removed from the third and subsequent issuings of the book. He remarked later to a friend that "I feel tremendously relieved that the season for success for *The Catcher in the Rye* is nearly over. I enjoyed a small part of it, but most of it I found hectic and professionally and personally demoralizing." Reviews of the novel were mixed, from out-and-out approval to questions about Salinger's attitudes, the colloquial style, the focus on an adolescent boy, and, of course, the issue which has since attracted attention-whether the book was fit for young readers. Thus *The Catcher in the Rye*, especially since issuance as a paperback in 1953, has been, curiously, both stipulated for and banned from high school and college reading lists (the foundation for, or lack of foundation for, such controversy is explored in the following pages of detailed analysis of the novel).

LIST OF SALINGER'S WORKS

The Catcher in the Rye, 1951; *Nine Stories*, 1953; *Franny and Zooey*, 1961; *Raise High the Roof Beam, Carpenters and Seymour: An Introduction*, 1963. (As indicated above, all subsequent works listed after *The Catcher in the Rye* are short stories, most of them published prior to collective issuance.)

A BRIEF LOOK AT SALINGER'S THEMES AND ATTITUDES

Following are some of the issues pertinent to any detailed analysis of Salinger's work, issues which are treated in the "Comments" below as well as in the short summary of what Salinger's critics have had to say about his writings: (a) His **protagonists** are often intelligent, sensitive, and very aware adolescents, or adults who, in either case, seek their own identity in relation to an external world with which they find themselves more or less at variance. (b) Alienation or disenchantment with the so-called "adult" world figures largely in Salinger's writings, often emphasized by rather "average" characters (parents, teachers, marriage partners, etc.) who interrelate with the troubled **protagonist**. (c) A definition of the "adult" world is sometimes sought or offered-it may be viewed as commercialized, materialistic, phony, ugly, grotesque-all suggestive of reasons for the sensitive **protagonist** to retreat from it, in reality or symbolically (for example, through madness, or suicide, or simply by introversion and fantasy). (d) Salinger is very concerned with the rather ancient question of innocence and experience in human lives, and how the life experience which is inevitable may best be realized instrue spiritual growth, instead of producing, say, a tough cynicism (such as that of Eloise in "Uncle Wiggily in Connecticut," or of young Selena and Eric in "Before the War with the Eskimos"). (e) Sometimes true "love" of humanity seems to be the solution offered, as in "Teddy". (f) Salinger's style includes a rather inspired use of detail - he can characterize in an instant's phrase - and a good deal of 20th-century slang, vocabulary of adolescents, colloquialisms.

THE CATCHER IN THE RYE

ACCLAIM

With the publication of *The Catcher in the Rye* in 1951, J. D. Salinger gained an almost immediate acceptance as being among the most significant post-World War II American novelists. Widespread critical acclaim, not without an element of protest, established the thirty-two-year-old novelist's reputation, and shortly thereafter his work became assigned reading for a majority of high school and college English courses. The esteem felt for him on campus and his appeal to the younger intellectual are quite understandable, for Salinger had begun the novel a full ten years before and had actually been writing for seventeen years. *The Catcher in the Rye* and the short stories that preceded it, therefore, appeal directly to youth, which the young author so imaginatively recreates.

It should not be thought that this story of the crises of a youthful **protagonist** was unique in American fiction, for *Huckleberry Finn* is certainly a prototype of Salinger's Holden Caulfield. Like Huck Finn, the deeply disturbed Holden Caulfield became a legendary figure, and his acute adolescent awareness became synonymous with the sensitivity of a great many young Americans.

THE CATCHER IN THE RYE

CHAPTERS 1-5

. . . .

CHAPTERS 1 AND 2

First Person

An element of prime importance to the effect that this novel has on the reader is the fact that it is told in the first person. The use of this method of telling a story lends verisimilitude to the details while, at the same time, the reader is made to feel that he knows more about what is happening than does the narrator. A major reason for the fact that *Huckleberry Finn* is the only literary sequel in history that surpasses its antecedent is that Huck was allowed to tell his own story, while Tom Sawyer's adventures were related by an adult. The result was that in *Tom Sawyer*, the author constantly interposes himself between Tom and the reader. We are told, instead of being allowed to discover for ourselves, what emotions it was intended that we feel in a given situation. We never really get to know Tom because we see him through the eyes of another person; when we read

Huckleberry Finn, it is almost as though we are living through his experiences ourselves.

The same is true in the case of Holden Caulfield. Because he is allowed to relate his own story in and on his own terms, we feel an empathy for him that could not have been otherwise achieved. The reader is granted an introspective view of the story; at the same time, because his background is not the same as Holden's, the reader retains his objectivity. Thus, he learns more about Holden than Holden himself knows.

Autobiography

A pitfall to be avoided is the conclusion that since many of the details about a fictional character agree with actual aspects of the author, the story is an autobiography. It is true that Pencey Prep reminds us of Valley Forge Military Academy-in Pennsylvania-which Salinger attended; it is true that Holden mentions an older brother who is a writer (who seems similar to Salinger himself) and to whom Holden always refers by his initials-D.B., not J.D.; there are, no doubt, many other characters and events that Salinger drew from his own life. It does not, however, necessarily follow that the story is autobiographical in every particular. Salinger follows the precepts of one accepted literary practice and writes about what he knows best. It is well known that A. Conan Doyle drew *Sherlock Holmes* from his own imagination, but it is to be doubted that Sir Arthur had a tithe of the adventures he so vividly described.

Holden's Honesty

Holden exhibits a cynical self-awareness as he retraces the events that led up to his present position. He has a good many strong opinions, yet he tries to look at both sides-or, in fact, the many sides-of a question, and, what is perhaps most important, he feels and tries to express his feelings. Holden's view of what is facile, unreflecting and cliche-ridden in the adult world is to figure largely in the rest of the novel. Holden's reaction-amusement rather than resentment-to the circumstances that cause his expulsion, is another indication of his innate honesty.

Holden's Language

Holden's colloquial - not to mention slangy - manner of speaking, as well as his boyish repetitions, stresses on certain words and his self-admitted vocabulary deficiencies all attract attention at first. In time, however, the reader is acclimated to Holden's narrative style. More important are Holden's reasons - that is to say, the author's reasons - for relating his story in such a manner. It is evident that the language of this account must remain consistent with the teenager who tells it. Holden's verbal limitations are related to the verities about him and about his world that emerge from this approach. Holden's account of what his teachers say and what his schoolmates say is also important. It is necessary that the reader accommodate himself to Holden's manner of speaking, if he is to understand the entire commentary of the novel.

The Importance Of Feelings

Holden's involvement with feelings is established early in the novel. His discussion of farewells is touching; moreover, it is important, since, from that discussion is adduced more information about various elements of Holden's personality. He is casual in his disclosure of matters that are surely important to him-his leaving school, for instance, or the theft of his personal belongings. We wonder whether or not Holden is keeping himself from feeling too strongly about things; or is he, perhaps, afraid to feel strong emotions? We may also speculate whether his indifference to people's opinions is not actually a means of hiding his fear that they won't like him.

Holden often searches for feelings; he tries to affect a sadness at leaving places, usually without success. This attempt to counterfeit emotions, and some of his apparently unmotivated antics give us further insight into his character. He would be the first to scoff at such a suggestion, but it is quite possible that Holden is trying to find himself.

Cynicism

Holden is cynical beyond his years, to an extent that may be quite disconcerting at first. Although we may feel that this cynicism is born of hidden insecurity and frustration, there is no gainsaying the fact that Holden's pithy comments are often apt and biting. In his account of his conversations with his teacher and the head of the school, the adults' remarks do not seem terribly profound. We can see that although they are well-meaning people, they tend to speak, as well as think, in cliches. There is an element of truth in what they say-cliches get to be cliches because the truths that they express are manifest-but that truth is rendered unpalatable for Holden by his inability to take these adults seriously. They represent the fatuousness and shallowness so often found in the middle-class world.

We say that Holden is "cynical beyond his years" advisedly. Because of Salinger's artistry, it is easy to forget that it is not a boy of seventeen who is telling this story, but an adult, and a perspicacious adult, at that. The language used is that of an intelligent, though troubled, boy; the wisdom and sentiments expressed are those of a worldly wise man.

"Black-And-White", Either/Or Thinking

One of the reasons adults and adolescents fail to communicate, as represented in Holden's exchange with Mr. Spencer, is the inflexibility of the rules and **conventions** of the adult world. Mind-sets, we might call them, a failure to perceive any middle possibilities between "either/or", a failure, in fact, to recognize the complexities of life.

Holden is on rather sound philosophical ground here. He is followingthetenetsofthefamousAmericanpsychologist-philosopher, William James, who regarded the universe as "pluralistic," that is, many-faceted, in spite of man's stubborn desire to classify and categorize it. Furthermore, according to James' philosophy, a person who admits this complexity, or the lack of neat "either/or's," is a pragmatist - that is, he is able to look at the world as it really is, even though this is less orderly, perhaps even frustrating in its lack of clear "yes or no" answers, and he is able to accommodate to changes in his world, whether external or in his own consciousness. We might be justified, therefore, in calling Holden Caulfield a pragmatist - a rather sophisticated and realistic thinker.

Emphasis On Facts

Despite his favorable qualities, Mr. Spencer demonstrates another aspect of adult inflexibility - that which overemphasizes factual knowledge. (Salinger's distaste for this method of educating young people seems to have expanded into a theory of education, stressing the desirability of showing rather than telling and labeling, so as not to stifle a person's naturalness or individuality; the story "Teddy" explores this theory.) With needless irritating repetition, Mr. Spencer dwells upon Holden's inadequate grasp of historical facts, but we are left with the feeling that Holden knows as much about ancient Egypt as he cares, or needs, to know.

One gets the impression that Mr. Spencer's approach to history is static rather than dynamic, that he stresses separate fragmented facts in a pedantic and uninteresting manner, and that he himself lacks historical perspective and has not even perceived how Egyptian history might be made interesting for his students so that they would be anxious to learn about it. Thus, Holden, in his awareness of the pluralistic universe that is being absorbed constantly into a new present, may be better equipped than Mr. Spencer to perceive reality. Yet, Holden is made to feel that he is wrong; he feels apologetic about his supposed inadequacies. This is bound to have unsalutary effects on his psychological well-being.

Health

The reader is given no specific diagnosis of Holden's ailments. Since he is telling the story while he is a resident of a rest home, we conclude that there is something wrong with him but we are never told what it is. This ambiguity is well executed by Salinger. He is aware that, in young people especially, there is a connection between physical and psychological health. Certainly Holden differs considerably from the traditional hero, who is physically and psychologically unblemished.

Mendacity

We find that one of the most oft-used words in Holden's lexicon is "phony." He is constantly detecting sham motives in the people around him. The advertisement for Pencey Prep disturbs him; the picture of a horse jumping over a fence gives in his opinion, a false image of the school. In Holden's judgment, Pencey is a home for dishonest, spoiled children, and not for idealized horsemen-to-be. Also held up to ridicule is the spurious picture of life that is found in Hollywood movies. Salinger's relationship with the movie industry was not extensive but it apparently left its mark. The reader may be reminded of the comments of other authors whose opinions of Hollywood were less than laudatory. S. J. Perelman called it "Bridgeport with palms" and P. G. Wodehouse referred to it as "Dottyville-on-the-Pacific."

Holden is deeply concerned with the fact that his older brother, D. B., has prostituted his writing talent by going out to California; he feels that D. B. is being untrue to himself and his convictions in his pursuit of material success. Holden thus exhibits his involvement with broad questions. This problem of the fate of talent, ideals and sensitivity in a materialistic society becomes one of Holden's preoccupations in the novel.

Communication

Salinger is concerned with the lack of communication in the adult world. An illustration of this is the magazine that Mr. Spencer tries to toss on the bed; he misses, and the magazine is picked up by Holden. The magazine, which falls to the floor, is meant, perhaps, to represent adult knowledge and experience; the "toss-and-miss" game demonstrates the lack of connection between the worlds of the adult and the adolescent.

Irony

Although Mr. Spencer regrets the necessity of giving Holden a failing mark, he cannot restrain himself from reading aloud Holden's inadequate examination composition. Thus, instead of assuaging the boy's discomfort, he adds to it. Holden, on the other hand, tries to alleviate the teacher's embarrassment by engaging him in aimless conversation. We see that their relationship is ironically inverted. Holden has more sympathy for and interest in people than does Mr. Spencer.

Holden's attempt to put his teacher at ease fails, in part, because although he has a great awareness, his immaturity precludes his channeling it into actual communication. Instead, Holden thinks, while chatting, about the ducks in Central Park. This delicate concern for the creatures of nature and sensitivity to the mysteries of nature are beyond Mr. Spencer's perspective ability. The teacher lives in another world.

Another ironic circumstance is exposed when Holden reminisces about Elkton Hills. The headmaster of Elkton Hills spoke only to those parents who had the proper social graces; the materialistic or naively factual aspects of the teaching profession are thus adduced. Holden is more attuned to reality than are his mentors, but he is incapable of handling his own world; nor are they capable of guiding him.

Holden leaves Mr. Spencer after consoling him and advising him not to worry, and the traditional image of the mild, harmless teacher has been established. We must realize, however, that Holden is also taking a one-sided view of things here. Mr. Spencer's failure to communicate and the Elkton Hills headmaster's hypocrisy are not necessarily the condition of the adult world, but Holden is too young and hypersensitive to see that, yet. In this sense there is a double **irony** in Holden's point of view.

CHAPTERS 3, 4 AND 5

Escapism

Holden is aware that he has a habit of lying and he ostensibly deprecates this fault. He is not entirely sincere in his self-castigation, however; he enjoys his fantasies, his imaginative escapes, and he is aware that his lies are of little significance. Salinger uses Holden's escapist tendencies to satirize the typical content of Hollywood movies; Holden projects himself into the unreal celluloid world by visualizing himself as the hero in a melange of typical Hollywood plots. We also see, here, a touch of exhibitionism in Holden; he cannot seem to help trying to draw attention to himself, even of people whom he does not particularly admire.

The Red Hunting Hat

The **theme** of escape through fantasy is continued when Holden toys with his red hunting cap. When Holden is interrupted in his reading, by Ackley, who interrogates him about the lost fencing equipment, he is annoyed and covers his face with the cap. He makes believe that he is blind and calls out to his mother to give him her hand. We can see that Holden is caught up and trapped in his own imaginary games. He wears the cap backward while he reads, thus asserting his own individuality; the cap thereby becomes a part of the fantasy world that he enters while reading, at the same time suggesting his own personal "hunting" or searching for companionship-with books or with real people.

Furthermore, the cap, because of its similarity to a baseball cap, probably reminds him of Allie's baseball mitt, and thus of Allie, and suggests ultimately the **theme** of the "catcher in the rye," or protector of childlike innocence and purity.

Status Seeking

The Cadillac-driving Mr. Ossenburger, after whom Holden's dormitory is named, is a typical representative of the status-seeking, mealy-mouthed middle class. Holden cannot take seriously the wealthy undertaker's sermon about God being our buddy, for he feels that the man's status and dignity are false. The expensive automobile, the financial donation to the school- for which the dormitory in his name is a quid pro quo- and his career of profiting on death all underscore Holden's mocking picture of adult society. Holden accuses the adult sermonizer of being too preoccupied with financial gain and his own status to be worthy of instructing others on religious or moral matters; this indictment could, of course, be applied to the large number of people who have merited it. This is a **theme** of Salinger's that recurs - in various guises - throughout his works. Salinger's characters that he seems most to admire are those who do not wish to appear to others any different than they are.

Holden's description of and reactions to the undertaker's inflated rhetoric are amusing, but they serve a more profound purpose; they deepen our appreciation of Holden's serious concerns and sharpen our vision of his abundant empathy. We can see just what it is that is contributing to turning Holden into the champion and protector of young innocence. Although we must always be aware of Holden's tendency to oversimplify, due to his own innocence, we cannot but respond to his horror of the crassness of the world and its social snobbery.

Ackley

It is not only the adult world that Holden finds displeasing; it is not a simple case of youth and age being mutually antagonistic. Ackley, an introvert, is depicted as being weird and nasty; his physical attributes are repugnant to boot. He is a social outcast at school, not only because of his poor grooming, but because he appears to be uncooperative and unfriendly. Being an introvert, he is driven more and more into himself because he is rejected. It is interesting to speculate on the fact that, despite their seemingly antithetical personalities, Holden and Ackley are alike in many respects. Neither boy is respected or accepted by his fellows. They both tend to withdraw into themselves and they both evince their lack of concern for the opinions of others-Holden by his iconoclastic capers and Ackley by his personal habits. We may come to the conclusion that the element in Holden's make-up that saves him from being as repellent to us as Ackley is Holden's native intelligence.

Stradlater

Perhaps nowhere in the world can unpleasant personal habits be more egregious than in school dormitory; Holden has already clearly delineated the disgust that Ackley fills him with. The case of Stradlater is a bit more complicated. Stradlater is representative of the athletically and socially successful boy whose accomplishments have gone to his head. Holden is upset by the disparity between appearance and reality; he feels that Stradlater is clean only on the surface and that underneath that surface he is a "secret slob." Ackley, on the other hand, makes no pretence of being anything but slovenly; at least he is not hypocritical about his personal habits.

Loneliness

Holden is hypersensitive to anything tawdry, and we see that he is repelled by the contrasting shapes that tawdriness can take in the persons of Ackley and Stradlater. Yet, in spite of his being critical of people, his loneliness draws him to them, and he really seeks companionship with both boys. Unfortunately, however, he can find no common ground on which to meet either boy.

Literature

Holden's conception of what constitutes great literature is an interesting one: that a great book, when read, will cause the reader to wish that he could telephone the author and talk to him. This is further evidence of Holden's desire for warmth and human relationship. This **theme** of a lonely youth searching for friendship, for deep personal relationships with his fellow man is central to this and, of course, to many other novels, It manifests itself in such diverse examples of the **genre** as Charles Dickens' *David Copperfield* and Nelson Algren's *The Man With The Golden Arm*.

Jane Gallagher

Salinger has a knack for allowing the reader a glimpse of an interesting character, but only, as it were, at second hand. Sometimes this can prove to be almost frustrating, as is true in the case of Jane Gallagher. From Holden's description of the way Jane plays checkers, with more regard for the symmetry of the pieces on the board than for the outcome of the game, we wish that she might have been introduced into the action of the novel.

In Holden's great fear of Jane's fate at the hands of Stradlater we find the seed of the "catcher in the rye" image. He wants to protect her innocence from the potentially corrupting influence of Stradlater. Thus, the lonely youth seeking to establish human companionship is simultaneously concerned with protecting innocence. The two activities work hand in hand.

Allie

The book's most delightful character never actually appears in the novel at all. Salinger uses a device similar to that of Truman Capote in his "Children On Their Birthdays" - the fact that a precocious child is no longer alive is the first thing the reader learns about that character; as the author fills in details about him, the reader's regret that he could not have met that character personally increases. The **episode** of Allie and the baseball glove is one of the most moving in the novel, for it beautifully conveys to us the extent of Holden's loss without violating the superficially offhand, sentimental tone that has been established as Holden's attitude toward the outside world.

Adult Distrust

An adult world that does not trust Holden because it cannot understand him is seen in the incident of the snowball. After making a snowball, Holden looks around for something to act as a target for it, but the snow-covered objects outside his window all look so pristinely lovely that he can't bring himself to destroy the symmetry of the beautiful scene. He carries the snowball to the bus, but when the bus driver refuses to believe that he does not intend to throw it, Holden feels defeated; in so many ways he is the soul of integrity and once again his integrity is questioned.

Another incident that is revelatory of the unsympathetic adult world revolves around Allie's death. Because Holden broke all the windows in the garage, and then tried to break the car windows, his parents spoke of sending him to a psychiatrist. The adult world cannot seem to understand the deep sense of loss that can be felt by an adolescent. Holden contrasts his lovely and likable little redheaded brother with the less attractive people surrounding him; this sharpens his already keen sense of bereavement. It is possible that Holden's recollections of Allie are colored by the fact that he is gone; nevertheless, we are quite willing to take Holden's word for it when he assures us that we would have liked Allie.

THE CATCHER IN THE RYE

. . . .

CHAPTERS 6, 7 AND 8

Ambivalence

Holden's feelings about Jane are ambivalent in two ways. He does not seem to be at all sure of what he wants their relationship to be, and he is equally unsure how Jane will conduct herself on a date with a self-acknowledged rake like Stradlater. It is typical of Holden that when he is unhappy, he seeks out the companionship of anyone who is close at hand-even the despised Ackley. (Careful reading, by the way, will disclose the fact that Salinger has inadvertently assigned two different names to Ackley's roommate. Possibly this was due to sections of two different versions of the story being subjoined. The best of authors occasionally err in this fashion-in *Huckleberry Finn* Tom Sawyer's girlfriend is called Bessie Thatcher, instead of Becky.)

It is difficult for us to take seriously Holden's confession of cowardice; he himself doesn't seem to be sure about it. We also do not know whether to list the results of Holden's encounter with Stradlater as a victory for the former or for the latter. Holden lost the physical battle, but he won a moral victory because he championed chivalry and virtue; he has been defeated but not dishonored.

Quixotism

As noted above, Holden attacks the cult of athletic prowess, whose motto is "might makes right."

His knightly behavior is redolent of the madness of *Don Quixote*, at least insofar as ideals are concerned; the battlefield is far more prosaic. This fight, which is like a duel, establishes Holden's quest to attain a moral order. (To be as fanciful as Holden himself, one might say that the red hunting cap, which he puts on backward, symbolizes a tarnhelm, the magical powers of which enable its wearer to become invisible.) Holden asserts himself as an adolescent caught between the anxiety of childhood and the hoped for assimilation into the adult world.

Generosity

Apparently, Holden cannot help being generous, no matter how unworthy are the recipients of his gifts. His willingness that almost amounts to an eagerness to oblige in granting favors-although he sometimes keeps caste by affecting reluctance-is indicative of his desperate need for fellowship. His generosity is not limited to material possessions-he gives of his time and company, often against his own inclinations.

Another aspect of Holden's generosity is his tendency to try to find some good in most people, even if only a miniscule amount. Thus, Stradlater's self-centeredness is transformed into the ability to keep a secret.

Alienation

Holden's departure from Pencey Prep is a recapitulation of a scene that he has played many times before, when he was forced to leave his temporary and shifting home, school. Still depressed about Jane's putative fate at the hands of Stradlater, he is rebuffed in his attempt to seek solace in conversation with Ackley. Salinger uses this inability to relate to a fellow student, a religious vocation or prep school to exemplify Holden's deep alienation from society. He cannot even go home to his family-at least, not yet; he puts it off as long as he can-because they will not understand him emotionally. Holden is thus driven more and more into himself, cut off from the social world; he reacts by putting on his childish symbol of escape and passivity, the red hunting cap.

Avoidance

Holden's chance meeting with the mother of a schoolmate leads him into the perpetration of another tangled skein of lies. Part of the psychological justification for this act-for which he feels remorse, even when committing it-arises from his inability to inflict pain; he does not want to make life difficult for people. This oversimplified easy way out appeals to his fertile imagination, but he seems to enjoy his imposture more than he should. (Note the resemblance to *Huckleberry Finn*; Huck could never come across a stranger without creating an entirely new autobiography for himself. He was often impelled to do this by reasons of self-preservation, but he seemed to enjoy himself mightily, too.)

Holden has the typical youthful predilection for feeling that he has the problems of the world on his shoulders, a natural concomitant of his view of himself as the focal point of all society. Thus, he feels responsible for far more situations than he could possibly control, let alone affect. Part of Holden's problem is that he has an overabundant supply of empathy, quite often for people who neither desire it nor appreciate it.

Acceptance

Holden's attempts to be accepted into the adult world are a bit ludicrous. Mrs. Morrow is apparently unimpressed by his talking about going for a drink or by his display of his prematurely gray hair. Like any other child, and like many an adult too, Holden has an overwhelming desire and need to be noticed.

Mothers

Salinger makes some trenchant observations about maternal affection and the blind spots it can cause. For all of Salinger's love-amounting at times almost to deification-of youthful innocence, he can see clearly how easily a mother's view of her children can be warped by love and pride. Of course, Salinger's comments are mild compared to what Philip Wylie has written on an allied subject; the latter's excoriating denunciation of what he termed "momism" is well known.

CHAPTERS 9, 10 AND 11

Companionship

More clearly than ever, we sense Holden's desperate need for companionship of almost any kind. His slip of the tongue in giving the cab driver his home address is revelatory of his subconscious desire to go home-although that particular repressed desire is vying within him with other, antithetical desires. That Holden is starved for companionship is revealed by the fact that many of the people with whom he attempts-or only considers the attempt-to strike up a conversation obviously have so little in common with him. This is even more clearly seen when he does elicit a response; the resulting conversation is usually perfectly inane.

Attraction Of Vulgarity

Holden's ambivalent nature is further adduced by his actions after he reaches New York. Although he is familiar with what we might call "the better things in life," he constantly manages to be drawn into vulgarity. (It is noteworthy that his familiarity with motion picture **cliches** is not consistent with his contempt for that medium.) With scores of hotels to choose from, he selects one that seems to be rife with perverts. He finds excuses not to call people he admires, but he telephones a girl he doesn't even know because he was told she was of easy virtue - and then he makes a botch of the conversation.

His continued quest for female companionship has similar results in the tawdry night club. His ideal of innocence and fun, Phoebe, with whom he hopes to find solace, is compared with these dull-witted girls who worship movie idols. Holden disdains and pities these vacuous creatures and yet he tries to prolong their stay in his company as long as possible. (Note that Salinger is guilty of an error in the nightclub scene: the legal minimum age at which one may consume liquor in New York is, and has been for many years, eighteen, not twenty-one.)

Phoebe And Jane

It is becoming apparent that there are only two females whose companionship Holden really enjoys. One is his ten-year-old sister and the other a girl with whom his relationship has been, in the main, platonic.

Phoebe is a delightful child; there are not many like her in literature, let alone in life. She has more than red hair in common with her brother Allie; she is charming, intelligent, vivacious and, most of all, fun. In fact, one might say that Salinger is eating his cake and having it too; he gave us the tragedy of Allie's death, but he brought him back to life in Phoebe.

We get the impression that insofar as he has ever been in love with any girl, Holden loves Jane. She can be trusted to share the innermost secrets of Holden's life, for example a look at Allie's glove. Jane is the book's only character who is Holden's age or older to whom Salinger does not impute a loss of innocence. However much he may care for Jane, though, Holden never lacks for an excuse to defer talking to or seeing her. There seems to be an integral part of Holden's psyche that refuses to allow him to find happiness.

CHAPTERS 12, 13 AND 14

Horwitz

Salinger's treatment of the interplay between the young boy and the hard-bitten cab driver is quite effective. Curiosity about the vagaries of nature is a leveling factor in man; to paraphrase Shakespeare, the love of nature makes the whole world kin. We see two kinds of innocence in contrast: Holden's youthful ingenuousness and the uneducated cabbie's simplicity. Horwitz is upset by Holden's questions at first, but soon his imagination is stimulated. Salinger deftly pokes fun at the myth of the omniscient New York cab driver by having Horwitz aver that he knows that fish are protected by Mother Nature; they eat through their pores while frozen in the lake. Perhaps Horwitz arrives at this conclusion so that he may feel secure in the knowledge that Mother Nature is looking after him.

Ernie

Because Ernie now seems so self-conscious in the tinselly atmosphere that he has surrounded himself with and because he now seems concerned only with projecting a flattering image of himself. Holden feels that Ernie-like D.B. - has knuckled under to the forces of crass materialism. This **theme** - the commercialization of art - exemplifies what Holden feels about the adult involvement with materialism that surrounds human acts and has the power to destroy anything worthwhile that man may create. The saddest thing about artists who succumb to the temptation of self-gratification is that they lose the ability to distinguish between art and entertainment.

Lillian

Lillian Simmons is another example of the shallowness of society. She cares more about being seen and heard that about communicating with people. Her motives and deceptions are so pitifully transparent that we must emulate Holden in his pity for her.

Sunny

Emotion is so important to Holden that he is appalled by the prospect of commercialized sex. While the physical aspects of love are very meaningful to him, they mean nothing if they are rendered impersonal and cold. Holden wants to talk with Sunny for a while; he wants to share her experiences and find out what made her what she is, but she is unable to respond. Once again he finds that people do not care about him as he would like to care about them. The encounter with the prostitute, showing first Holden's brash temerity, followed in turn by misgivings, qualms and then horror of the vulgarity of the situation, is well delineated. It serves to reinforce the image we have of Holden as an innocent youth being initiated into the cold and calculating world of the adult society.

Religion

In the increasing seriousness of his reflections, Holden ponders on religion. He evinces a pragmatic bent in such matters; his value judgments of the Disciples are from a strictly twentieth-century point of view. Christ is accepted by Holden as a pure ideal, but the lesser representatives of Christianity are, as

Holden sees them, the frail human element that corrupts. Thus, they are harsher judges of their fellow man than God would be.

Maurice

Although Holden has certainly told more than his share of lies, he has a very definite code of honor; he lives up to it and he expects other people to live up to theirs. When Holden faces up to Maurice, it is not for the sake of the money - as we have seen, Holden does not know the value of money - but because Holden cannot abide that kind of dishonesty. Salinger has taken great pains to prepare the reader for Holden's courageous stand. Holden has previously admitted that he is not physically aggressive, and because he shies away from fights he considers himself to be a coward. This battle, however, involves truth; consequently, Holden abandons all precautions. It is a moral conflict fought out in a most unconventional setting. Although Holden loses the physical encounter with Maurice he has successfully defended his honor.

Fantasy

After the fight, Holden takes refuge in the world of fantasy. It is interesting to note that this lad, who despises the fraudulent celluloid world, often thinks in terms of Hollywood images. Salinger seems to be satirizing a world that is becoming unable to distinguish reality from fantasy - a world in which an actor who plays a doctor on television receives countless letters begging him for medical advice.

CHAPTERS 15 AND 16

Materialism

We find that Holden is not afflicted with pride in material possessions; the philosophy of "conspicuous consumption" means nothing to him. He tells us of the time when he was embarrassed because his suitcases were so much nicer than his roommate's. Displaying his characteristic empathy, Holden tried to hide his suitcases, in consideration of his roommate's feelings. This thoughtful act did not achieve its desired effect, however, because his roommate wanted the suitcases to be seen so that it would appear as though he owned them. This simple tale illustrates the entire process of jockeying for a superior materialistic image in our society. It is not necessary actually to own things; the appearance of ownership suffices. At about the time that Salinger was writing this book, people who could not afford Cadillacs (the status symbol par excellence) were buying tail fins to make their Chevrolets look like Cadillacs; people who did not own television sets were putting dummy television antennas on their roofs.

Charity

The nuns have not fallen victim to this false philosophy; they stand for a measure of self-sacrifice that extends far beyond the "society charities," which Holden feels are all based on self-indulgence. This conflict between true charity-or a total commitment-bothers the youthful **protagonist**. He rejects internal self-gratification as a fraud and demands that false ego be purged. Of course Holden himself is not being entirely consistent here, since the money that he gave the nuns meant nothing to him, but it must be admitted that he did for them what he could. Holden feels that money is a demeaning influence on society-or, as the New Testament has it, "The love of money is the root of all evil."

Salinger is telling us that a charitable act is deserving of the name only if the performer of the act is giving up something that he values and getting nothing in return. When Mr. Ossenburger donated money to Pencey, for instance, it was not charity; his name was immortalized-or so it would have seemed to him-on the dormitory building. Thus, he was making a simple purchase. The egotism behind a charitable act destroys the value of the act, reducing it to self-gratification.

Sally Hayes

Holden's masochism manifests itself again when he seeks out Sally Hayes. She is attractive and superficially intelligent, but she does not have the qualities that Holden most admires-emotional profundity and an involvement with people. He further flagellates himself by taking her to places he does not like, among people he detests.

The Poor Family

When Holden follows the poor family along the street, it shows his subconscious quest for home life, and a spiritual father. Holden's mention of his father is conspicuous by its almost total absence from the novel. He has said that his father is quite wealthy but also quite busy; they do not seem to share many experiences. This lack of affection from his father has a profound effect on Holden's life. Psychologists might say that he is failing in his school work in order to gain the attention of his father and to command his father's love. This partial explanation has a bearing on the plot as well as on other events and circumstances that contribute to Holden's failure. Nevertheless, he is responsible for his own deeds, no matter how mitigating the circumstances may be. Holden must contrive to channel this responsibility in a meaningful direction. To bridge the gap between adolescence and manhood demands an assimilation of values and experiences that are at present but a jumble to Holden. The process has been and is going to be slow and painful.

This poor family represents innocence to Holden - the child is singing just "for the hell of it." There is no sense of shame attached to his actions; a spiritual purity surrounds his singing. The song itself becomes identified with Holden's desire in life, as we shall see later.

Mutability

When Holden searches for Phoebe, one of the first places he goes is to the museum. He recalls the days when he attended her school and he recollects the occasions when he visited the museum. The nostalgia of childhood remembrances gives him a warm feeling, but he recognizes, perhaps for the first time, that many years have passed and things are no longer the same. He is older now; he is a different person. Although Phoebe is going to the same school and the same museum, her experiences, in varying degrees, will differ from his. This realization has a profound effect on Holden. Change-mutability-is a reality. Life goes on and the past seems quite distant to him now. The transitory quality of life makes him realize that he is not a child anymore. His decision not to enter the museum is different from previous occasions in the novel when he backed away from an experience; he really no longer has the urge to enter. It does not appeal to him now. He cannot go home again to the world of childhood; he must cross the threshold into the world of adulthood.

Salinger expands on the desirability of immutability when he describes the various exhibits in the museum and notes the comforting fact that they never change. A boy could grow into manhood, marry and have children of his own, or even grandchildren, but the same Eskimo would still be fishing through the same hole in the ice. The exhibits are thus an expression of immortality in a mortal world. Poets have, of course, long dilated on this and similar themes. In "The Rubaiyat of Omar Khayyam" we find:

Come, fill the Cup, and in the fire of Spring Your Winter-garment of Repentance fling: The Bird of Time has but a little way To flutter - and the Bird is on the Wing.

The seventeenth-century English poet Andrew Marvell, in his "To His Coy Mistress," said:

But always at my back I hear Times winged chariot drawing near, And yonder all before us lie Deserts of vast eternity.

The latter poet's solution, incidentally, was not to keep fleeing ineffectually, but to turn the tables and make "time run," or in short, to seize each new day and live it vigorously and affirmatively.

THE CATCHER IN THE RYE

CHAPTERS 17–26

....

CHAPTERS 17, 18 AND 19

Sincerity

Superficial social engagements are repellent to Holden, but he continually makes and keeps them. He cannot understand why he blurts out that he loves Sally; he almost convinces himself that it is true at the time, but in his heart he knows that it is not. His desire to be sincere is forever trapping him and leading him to be quite insincere.

The conversation at the theatre annoys him greatly because it seems to contain cultural involvement and great significance; in reality, as Holden knows, it is hollow and trivial. The audience at the theatre is like a large portion of the audience at an opera or concert; they go not to hear the music but to engage in a contest to see who can be the first to destroy an emotion-filled moment with premature applause.

The lack of true warmth in social relationships disturbs Holden because he desires to love, to be an adult, to be a person who is committed emotionally and psychologically to another person.

Search For Stability

Sally's desire for admiration of her physical attributes leads Holden and Sally to a popular skating rink where their efforts to ice-skate are ludicrous. Since they are both very poor skaters they are forced to give up the social pretense and leave the ice. In the ensuing conversation-as well as throughout the novel-Holden seeks to be understood by and establish a relationship with a female. He is searching for stability. But the more he tries to explain to Sally whence comes his dissatisfaction with his life, the more he becomes unrealistic and confusing. His request that Sally run off with him would have offended a far more understanding person than she. This romantic request illustrates his urge to break through **conventions** and be an adult, but it is indicative of how childish he still is.

Holden's almost incoherent conversation with Sally articulates his disenchantment with the adult world and its demands and conformities. As such, it is a fairly compact account of the complaints of many of Salinger's protagonists, adolescent and adult, as seen in *Nine Stories*. They are all unhappy in a world they never made.

Escape

Although Holden desires stability and is willing to commit himself to a meaningful life he cannot bring himself to compromise his ideals. He still wants to escape what he would call a "phony" future; he wants no part of the settled life of the ordinary college graduate - the routine quest for material acquisitions. Sally, of course, cannot comprehend all this - it is, after all, Holden's personal crisis-so their parting is unhappy and angry. Their argument ends Holden's attempts for the moment to establish this kind of relationship.

Values In Entertainment

The great majority of movies-foreign, as well as American-create an unreal world that Holden finds unacceptable. The story of the particular movies recounted by Holden, is a glorification of material success in typical soap opera fashion; false sorrows and happy endings are strewn about with a lavish hand. Holden refuses to be overwhelmed by the sheer weight of the stage show; he would rather pay attention to personal, individual performances. For example, he believes that Jesus would also hate the meretricious Christmas show but He would appreciate the orchestra's tympani player. Holden's brother Allie liked that musician so much he sent him a postcard from Washington, D.C. To appreciate an unsensational but profoundly true performance is a beautiful thing, in Holden's eyes. This, of course, is diametrically opposed to the philosophy of the mass media, which glorifies the sensational and false.

Carl Luce

Carl knows a great deal about relationships with women, but only the physical aspects. He is an expert on sex, not love. He rebuffs Holden's attempts to engage him in a personal and serious conversation and continues to play the role of the superior being who is the final arbiter on any matter he wishes to discuss. His spurious intellectualism can be discerned through

Holden's remarks. When they were at school, Carl saw that his informal seminars on sex were dispersed when he was tired; he wanted to make sure that no conversations took place while he was absent, so that he would continue to be the one that everyone sought when they desired information on any aspect of sex, homosexual or heterosexual. Carl loved to play the oracle, but he was never a sincere intellectual who gloried in the give and take of discussion and who admired genuine inquiry and developing self-awareness. He wanted control of any situation by being in possession of all the "facts." Salinger caricatures this type of knowledge by having Holden inform us that Carl had a large vocabulary, the best at school; or, at least, so indicated the tests. The lack of relationship between good marks and genuine character and personal development is the horror implicit in many modern educational practices.

Spiritual Experience

The only common ground found between Carl and Holden is their agreement that sex is both a physical and a spiritual experience. (It must be admitted, of course, that Holden has no first hand knowledge about the matter, as yet.) This idea excites Holden, who asks if this is why Carl now has an Eastern girlfriend. The lack of unity of the physical and spiritual elements in Holden's life is at the core of his own basic problem. Nevertheless, the middle ground between these two extremes of human attraction is man's abode, just as Holden is caught between childhood and adulthood, between anxiety and assimilation.

Carl advises Holden to undergo psychoanalysis; this is a **foreshadowing** of Holden's real needs. He informs Holden that he himself does not need analysis because he has adjusted to life through his father's advice. Holden proceeds to punish himself-in response to amorphous guilt feelings-by getting drunk. In his musings concerning guilt and sadness he arrives again at thoughts concerning Allie's death. Perhaps Salinger is saying here that Holden, being an impressionable adolescent, holds himself responsible for not being able to prevent death; this is why he fails in school and cannot abide institutions. In order to eschew culpability he tries to pass himself off as an adult, but he is not accepted as one because of his youthful mannerisms.

Quest For Answers

In this internal quest of Holden Caulfield, we see his burgeoning preoccupation with the mysteries of life. He is searching for the answers to profound questions-his curiosity concerning where the ducks in the park go in winter time symbolizes his desire to learn the way nature functions and, by extension, the secrets of nature. When he escapes into fantasy through his imaginary bullet wound we see the natural processes of solace, relief and escape from pain that come through the exercise of imagination. Holden is lonely and depressed; he feels sorry for his mother and father, especially his mother who, he feels, has yet to get over Allie's death.

CHAPTERS 20, 21 AND 23

Hunter And Hunted

Holden's red hunting cap seems to symbolize both the hunter and the hunted - that is, Holden's seeking life and being pursued by it. His fantasy of being wounded has some reality about it since it is becoming manifest that he is headed for the nervous breakdown that was hinted at earlier, because of the conflicts between idealism and reality, and because of his inability to assume control over his hitherto purposeless life. The hunting cap represents his passive resistance to many unpleasant aspects of life; he bought it when his schoolmates ostracized him and he dons it whenever he wants to retreat from unpleasant happenings.

Home

His decision to sneak home to Phoebe shows us his tremendous desire to be at home again and thus establish a relationship with someone he can love and will love him. He realizes that his pathological introversion is becoming dangerous to his mental and spiritual health. His recollection of the rain falling at Allie's funeral gives a glimpse into his ironic thoughts; in his deep sorrow he speculated on the people, who should feel privileged at being among the living, running for cover from the rain.

Catcher In The Rye

One of the most important and revealing sections of the novel involves Holden's arrival at his home. At last Holden is beginning to formulate his thoughts - a bit incoherently, it is true - about what he wants to do with his life. The "catcher in the rye" is the guardian of innocence and the protector of innocents. Thus, we discern Salinger's oft - implied creed - the human animal is pure in his childhood; he is not corrupted until he enters adult society. Whatever unpleasant characteristics a child may display are the results of premature exposure to adult influence - which may remind us of Holden's prematurely gray hair. This idea is a slight variation of Rousseau's concept of the "Noble Savage."

We can see Holden's great attachment to Phoebe's childish innocence and preternatural wisdom. She wants to protect

Holden and also make him grapple with his responsibilities. Salinger artistically juxtaposes Phoebe's smallness against the enormous furniture of the room-D.B.'s-she chooses to sleep in. The large, venal world and the small, innocent child are symbolic of the problems that Holden must learn to face.

Insight

The arguments against the usefulness of school that Holden presents to Phoebe represent the visceral insight that he has been developing during the course of the novel. He sees himself as a romantic hero challenging the institutionalized academic ogre. He is depressed at the thought that he may prove unequal to the struggle; he does not want to become what we call today an "organization man."

Conception Of Good

When Phoebe challenges Holden to name something that he thinks is good, he thinks of the nuns. Their spiritual dedication to the cause of charity is summed up physically for Holden in their black habits and the steel-rimmed glasses of one them. In his eyes, the physical and spiritual are united in their total commitment. Holden is not aware that although the nuns were not motivated by materialistic status-seeking, they were not altogether free of spiritual status-seeking in their motivations. Holden is impressionable; he follows his moral instincts in his evaluation of people.

When asked what he wants to be, he is unable to think of a practical occupation. He answers by telling what he wants to do with his life, in broad general terms; he cannot envision becoming something other than what he is now. His philosophy does permit him to choose here and now to do something in the future. His choice involves the key image of the novel; he wants to be the catcher in the rye, to save innocent children from falling into the abyss of adult corruption. He yearns for philosophical significance in his life to have a great moral purpose above and beyond practical truths. The mission takes on the godlike proportions of a savior. Without sacrilegious intent, he wishes to save humanity from the evil of its ways.

Identification

Salinger uses a clever device by having Phoebe demonstrate her belching ability immediately after Holden states his philosophy. This absurd juxtaposition of the lofty and the mundane serves to heighten the mood of the profound situation that Salinger is depicting. The technique lends verisimilitude to the novel and enables the reader to identify Holden's world with his own. Salinger's artistry causes the novel to be a mature work of art, and not merely a book for youngsters. At the same time, of course, young people find the novel eminently enjoyable and understandable. Being closer to Holden's age, they may find it easier to identify with him and his problems.

Central Image

As we have said, the key to the meaning of the novel is in the image of the "catcher in the rye." The actual line of Burns' poem is "if a body meet a body," but Holden does not have the exact words, although he has the words that interest him. His mishearing of the words may be symbolic of his incapacity to perceive reality accurately - that is, respond to the world as it really is, rather than as he wishes it were. However, careful reading will disclose that, as Holden relates the story, he is aware that he had the wrong words and that Phoebe is correct in telling him that it was "meet." Thus, Salinger is indicating that Holden has a new-found ability to come to terms with reality. Holden has changed, as we shall see in our perusal of the remainder of the book.

Family Relationships

Holden, who likes to dance, says the Phoebe is a wonderful dancer. Her ability to perform this social ritual has a great significance for Holden; it is one of the innocent pleasures of life that he likes to recall. In its way, perhaps, it is a way to participate in the pleasures of the adult world. In any event, he and Phoebe can perform together very well. They have an ability to exercise their talents in a harmonious and disciplined manner. This fact is important for proper comprehension of the novel-Holden needs Phoebe; his relationship with her will serve as a basis for a solution to his problems.

While Holden is with Phoebe, Mrs. Caulfield appears for the first and only time in the novel. Holden has spoken about her; we learn that she is kind, but somewhat insecure. A poor sleeper whose worry and concern is constant, she has never really recovered from her grief at Allie's death. Her reaction to Phoebe's (supposed) smoking is the only evidence we see that she can display parental authority. Her reproof is surprisingly mild; Salinger cloaks her response in ambiguity. It could mean that she is being psychologically clever by not attaching too much importance to Phoebe's act, but this seems doubtful. It could be evidence of laxness on her part, or perhaps gratification that

Phoebe did not take refuge in a lie (which, if true, is ironic because Phoebe did lie). Mrs. Caulfield's sense of parental responsibility cannot really be judged from this specific instance because it is inconclusive; but an overall observation is permissible. Phoebe said she smoked because she was unable to sleep, which might indicate that she was psychologically or physically uncomfortable. Once she finds that Phoebe is warm enough and therefore physically comfortable, Mrs. Caulfield makes no further effort to learn whether Phoebe is lonely for disturbed in any way. On the surface, it would seem that Mrs. Caulfield does not try to give her children psychological or spiritual warmth. She seems to be somewhat troubled herself-she has constant headaches - and not very capable of spiritual understanding. Holden may have been driven to the refuge of hypersensitivity by his parent's incapable handling of his problems.

/e4 The Lie:

Phoebe's lie to her mother about smoking poses an interesting moral question: should one condone or condemn her behavior? The answer would depend on one's attitude toward Holden. If he is conceived of as a wrongdoer who deserves to be caught, Phoebe should have told the truth; if one has sympathy for Holden's plight, the conclusion is that Phoebe told a sweet, unselfish lie.

The moral dilemma presented here parallels that of Huck Finn, when he protects the runaway slave by telling a lie. Huck castigates himself afterward and believes that he is doomed because of his lie; the reader, however, knows better. Mark Twain, who was always closely associated with the philosophy of the lie, also wrote a short story called "Was It Heaven-Or Hell," in which the question of the moral acceptance of the precept of an "unselfish lie" is thoroughly threshed out.

In *The Catcher in the Rye* the problem is not germane to an appreciation of the entire novel, but it does have relevance. In order properly to evaluate Holden Caulfield, one must ask oneself where moral responsibility resides-in the individual or in society. Certainly, the complex interrelationship of the two makes a simple solution impossible; Salinger wisely leaves the decision to the reader.

Phoebe And Holden

In addition to the moral problem raised here, which permeates the entire novel, one can see a direct contrast between Phoebe and Holden. Holden tells lies in order to escape painfully embarrassing situations, at times, but more often his lies are completely purposeless. Phoebe's lie has a tangible motivation; she is more down to earth than is Holden. Phoebe is responsible person who uses the device with continence and deliberateness.

When Phoebe asks Holden to promise to see her play and he acquiesces, one sees his final resolution adumbrated. Holden loves his little sister, and does not want to hurt her.

Catharsis

It is this love for Phoebe - and, really, for his entire family - that causes Holden to break into cathartic tears. Phoebe has given him her Christmas gift money, and he is leaving home. This ambivalent exit-he is unable to make up his mind whether or not he really wants to be caught-is preceded by a symbolic gesture; Holden gives his red cap to Phoebe. The reason he now eschews the hat, which has been symbolic of his passive - though rebellious - idealism lies in Holden's realization that his quest for moral responsibility is over, in a sense; the quarry has been sighted and he no longer needs his hunting cap.

CHAPTER 24

Mr. Antolini

The story comes full circle when Holden again seeks contact with a figure of authority as embodied by a teacher. His visit to Mr. Antolini parallels the events in the opening section of the novel, when Holden visits Mr. Spencer, Mr. Antolini is much younger than Spencer; he is a very articulate man and very much in contact with reality.

Just as Salinger used separate bedrooms as a device to symbolize the lack of communication between Mr. and Mrs. Spencer, he implies, a lack of communication between Mr. and Mrs. Antolini by having them always shouting at each other from different rooms in their apartment; they are rarely found in the same room. This distance between man and wife is an aspect of the loneliness and isolation that Holden often perceives in life. Mr. Antolini's psychic struggles are denoted by his chain smoking and heavy drinking; he is not as impervious to the vicissitudes of life as we had first thought.

Theories Of Education

Holden tries to explain to Mr. Antolini why he failed school. Emerging from his almost incoherent discourse is his distaste for arbitrary rules. Mr. Antolini argues that there must be some order, that there is a time and a place for everything, but Holden points out that sometimes the realization of just what interests a person is born when that person is talking about something else entirely. This approach to the positive through the negative shows Holden's acute perception. He concludes that the speech teacher, Mr. Vinson, was very intelligent but was not possessed of "much brains." This is further evidence of Holden's (or Salinger's) acute perception. The thesis is, of course, that wisdom is superior to mere intelligence; wisdom is the use and application of intelligence in a compassionate manner.

Thus summed up is a major portion of Holden's problems at school. He believes that wisdom is -or should be - the school's primary concern. Knowledge should make one happier and wiser; the information he received at school did not make Holden happier and was, therefore, not knowledge in its truest sense.

Advice

Mr. Antolini warns Holden that the youth is heading for a fall; this foreshadows Holden's breakdown and echoes the symbol of catching children as they fall over the cliff. The physical manifestation of Holden's collapse is his increasing inability to concentrate and his nagging headache.

Mr. Antolini's advice to Holden is epitomized in his quotation of Wilhelm Stekel, the psychiatrist:

The mark of the immature man is that he wants to die nobly for a cause, while the mark of the mature man is that he wants to live humbly for one.

This affirmative advice is quite applicable to Holden's case; to accept this philosophy would mean to accept, in a constructive way, his role in the world. Thus far, of course, Holden has not accepted life; he has, instead, rebelled against school and family in the "immature" spirit of "dying nobly for a cause."

Search For Truth

Since the plot of the novel revolves around school - and thereby knowledge - it is fitting that a teacher should discuss Holden's attitude toward learning. As Mr. Antolini says, Holden is in love with knowledge; this is true but, as was said above, Holden rejects the educational system because it does not help him in his passionate search for truth. This search is one of the major **themes** of the novel - that is, Holden's quest for wisdom, in order to establish a moral order by asserting himself. Holden's involvement with moral and intellectual truth renders him vulnerable to the false and unjust elements of life.

Mr. Antolini's Gesture

Mr. Antolini has asked Holden about the state of his acquaintanceship with girls. Holden's response, which deprecates Sally's worth and shows a renewed interest in Jane, evinces his willingness to attempt to establish a mature relationship with a girl. It is a natural question for Mr. Antolini to ask, but the aftermath makes it seem more dramatic, in retrospect.

We are never quite sure just why Mr. Antolini came and put his hand on Holden's head while the boy was asleep. Salinger is deliberately ambiguous about the matter and it must be admitted that the point is not a vital one. If Mr. Antolini is a homosexual, that fact only serves as ironic comment on his sound moral advice. If he is not, and Holden mistook the import of the gesture, it is further evidence of how Holden's hypersensitivity adds to his difficulty in entering into honest human relationships.

CHAPTERS 25 AND 26

Note

The last section of the book is probably the fullest in content and the tightest in structure. Because the **themes** are resolved as the novel comes to its conclusion, any interpretation of the events and symbols of the entire novel will depend on a close reading of this section.

Awareness

Holden's second thoughts about Mr. Antolini indicate an emerging awareness. After he casts doubt on his early conclusions as to what had occurred at the apartment, Holden is forced to concede that Mr. Antolini showed true charity to him, giving of his time and attention, regardless of the interpretation that might be placed on his later actions. As usual, Holden is capable of seeing more than one side of a matter.

Never To Return Home

Holden next decides that he will never return home. Spiritually, at least, it is true that he will never return home because he is undergoing the profound metamorphosis from adolescence to maturity; he will never return to childhood nor will he escape any more into the world of fantasy. He must go forward and grow up and thus break away from his emotional attachment to the past.

Fantasy

With characteristic ambivalence, Holden, while preparing to enter the adult world, indulges in fantastic daydreams. His dream of escaping from reality as an anonymous deaf-mute to an idyllic cabin in the woods mirrors the romantic dreams of the poets. His vision of the beautiful and unreal girl he will marry is typical of his sentimental solutions to the problems of life.

Vice

Holden's wish to say goodbye to Phoebe brings him to the school that he attended years ago. Ironically, this attempted farewell will lead him home as well as to the destruction of his false conception of the ideal of childhood innocence. The obscene graffiti he discovers on the walls of the school, he mistakenly assumes are the work of perverted adults. His inability to perceive that children are responsible contains a certain amount of pathos; he is so anxious to defend the pristine purity of childhood-to be the catcher in the rye. There is further **irony** in Holden's mistaken equation of vulgarity with vice. He is too ready to assume that innocence is capable to being corrupted with a word.

The Tomb

Holden's touching concern for children is seen in his conversation with the boys he meets at the museum. When he tells them all about Egyptian mummies, he is making use of, in a very practical way, the knowledge he gained in Mr. Spencer's history class. This is an amusing link to the opening section of the book-at last Holden finds that those hard-won facts are of some use.

The two boys are frightened and run away from the Egyptian tomb; it is quite appropriate that they should fear the mysterious and the unknown. Holden's fear is of the unknown-to him-adult world, and of the brutality and violence he is sure is there. Left alone, Holden sees the same obscene phrase in the tomb itself, causing him to speculate on the ubiquity of vulgarity; he feels that it will accompany him to his grave.

Climax

Phoebe's arrival marks the dramatic conclusion of the novel. She is wearing the red cap, thus symbolically changing places with Holden. Now it is Phoebe who acts irresponsibly and irrationally, by wanting to run away; Holden perforce becomes the apostle of common sense. Thus, Phoebe-presumably unwittingly-becomes the catalytic agent that causes Holden, willy-nilly, to accept responsibility.

Conclusion

Holden had told us at the beginning of the book that he would tell us no more than he had told D.B.; he has done this, and we know now the events that precipitated his breakdown. True to his word, Holden will say no more. We may recall that at the conclusion of *Huckleberry Finn* Huch says:

... there ain't nothing more to write about, and I am rotten glad of it, because if I'd 'a' knowed what a trouble it was to make a book I wouldn't 'a' tackled it, and ain't a-going to no more.

These seem to be Holden's sentiments, exactly.

THE CATCHER IN THE RYE

. . . .

HOLDEN CAULFIELD

The central character and the sole source of information for the events in the book. We learn everything only as it comes through Holden, the narrator and **protagonist**. In general, Holdens environment can be considered unstable and superficial. He rejects the traditions of school because they are artificial, lacking depth and warmth. His loneliness and rebellion come from his passive rejection of the false **conventions** and materialistic values that surround him. Because Holden fails in school, uses vulgar expressions, gets drunk, and is very interested in sex we might consider him to have low moral standards. Although these common adolescent characteristics may not fit in with our idealistic conception of a teen-ager, Holden represents the lonely American youth seeking to establish a moral code based on transcendent values. Holden's wealthy background, however, allows him to skip over all the middle-class materialistic concerns of our society. Holden's ambition to be the "catcher in the rye" symbolizes his desire to establish a moral order. (His name is a pun upon this **theme**: "hold" in "field.") Humorous as well as honest but by no means perfect, Holden searches for some purposeful relationship, but he is not yet prepared for an adult role in society.

His interest in everything stems from his youthful search for experience and freedom. This general but undefined interest in things demonstrates his undeveloped sensibilities. It is important to realize that other characters can be seen and understood only through this sensibility, i.e., Holden's consciousness is the consciousness of the entire novel-characters emerge only as they mirrored in this consciousness. On the surface we know only what Holden tells us about these people.

Is he defeated by society or will he change society? His general breakdown may have been brought about by society, but it does lead him back to reality with a new awareness. Holden's new awareness, however, will not change society. Like Huck Finn, Holden is a youth whose social significance must be evaluated in practical terms. Huck Finn did not establish racial equality everywhere, and Holden Caulfield does not give society a moral vision that transcends the false power and false security that materialism offers as the raison d'etre of our society. What he does gain for himself is the recognition that no man is an island.

PHOEBE CAULFIELD

She epitomizes the child prodigy type that Salinger so frequently creates. Her childish whimsy is mixed with serious perceptions that force Holden to reevaluate his actions and probe his conscience. In the novel, Phoebe receives Hiden's full esteem, as she represents the continued flow of children who must be cared for, the life process that is man's responsibility. Her unselfishness stems from a basic innocence which Holden understands but which overwhelms him.

ACKLEY

He is neither ambitious nor generous. Rather, Ackley is an unfriendly, unsophisticated youth who reacts with scorn because he does not fit into society. His character is drawn to perfection by Salinger. His reaction to alienation contrasts with Holden's. The apathy and cynicism he express cover up his deep resentment at his rejection by society.

ALLIE CAULFIELD

Salinger creates another off-stage prodigy. Allie is another of the near perfect, precocious, young people who populate his fiction. He functions almost as an alter ego to Holden who compares everything to him.

MR. SPENCER

He yearns to be sympathetic but fails. He represents an older generation of sweet but befuddled teachers who have lost contact with the realities of life. In Holden's eyes he would be classed as a nice but depressing guy.

Mr. Spencer's genuineness as a person can be seen beneath his fumbling ways. The Indian blanket that he and his wife bought on a vacation symbolizes his sincere but simple delights. The Indian blanket also shows his honest but uncommunicable love of history and culture.

MR. ANTOLINI

A younger man who left the Elkton Hills school to teach at N.Y.U., he is more articulate than Spencer, and thus is able to communicate a good deal with Holden and show him how even idealism can be put to constructive rather than self-destructive use, and how necessary it eventually becomes to reach some compromise with the rest of the world, however vulgar it seems, and to establish some order within oneself. It is one of Holden's more significant lessons that, though Mr. Antolini may not be perfect, he can be helpful. Thus, this teacher weakens Holden's tenacious grip on the either/or reasoning that often results in a paralysis of action, or in escapism.

STRADLATER

There has to be such a character in order to suggest all the qualities in American society that Holden despises, from the exaggerated evaluation of athletic ability and masculine parade of virility to personal egotism, superficial even callous thinking, worship of materialism and amoral ethical position. Stradlater, though, is popular, successful with girls, a leader of boys; he is not, however, a person to be looked up to according to the more subtle but more desirable standards Salinger details in his writings.

SALLY HAYES

For the most part she is representative of the wealthy, superficial world of Holden's own background. Through knowing her, he learned how to distinguish a surface knowledge and culture from true depth and understanding. Certainly he is not able to communicate to Sally any of his deepest problems.

[There are of course other lesser but interesting characters, particularly those mentioned who appear little, if at all: Jane Gallagher; Mr. and Mrs. Caulfield; Allie, the near-perfect dead brother.]

THE CATCHER IN THE RYE

The pattern of Salinger's fiction - and therefore the approach which critics take toward it - is generally that of a "misfit" hero, child or adult, caught up in a world that emerges as both meretricious and virtuous. Many of these **protagonists** themselves are a mixture of deplorable, mean qualities and appealing, often tender-comic innocence. Thus Salinger's "dramas," such as *The Catcher in the Rye* and the pieces in Nine Stories, often enact the conflict of such heroes (both an internalized and an externalized conflict) as they try to accommodate - which does not always mean "adjust" - to their world. And significantly - it is a major **theme** of Salinger's, - there is often a crucial moment (what James Joyce termed an "epiphany" or revelatory and changing experience) for these characters, a kind of conversion through compassion, trust and love, which saves them from real or symbolic death and suggests that they may henceforward be able to function more adequately in their world.

THE MISFIT HERO

This misfit hero is variously approved or disapproved of by critics, as superior or inferior or in between. (The term "misfit hero" can be credited to Paul Levine, incidentally, who has traced the whole development of such a **protagonist** in Salinger's work.) Criticism of the misfit hero depends upon how favorably or unfavorably his inevitable alienation from his world is regarded. Some critics - Mary McCarthy - for one, condemn his disenchanted retreat as smug or even childish rather than childlike (the first term puts the blame more upon the **protagonist**; the second implies it is society's fault). Warren French points out that Seymour Glass, by many of his actions in "A Perfect Day for Bananafish," seems to be demanding attention in a childish way (which of course suggests insecurity and a need for love). He disrupts the composure of adults, as French puts it: "How would most people react to being accused of staring at a nonexistent tattoo? How would people react to a man so disrespectful of age and femininity as to ask a grandmother about her plans for passing away? - to a man so disrespectful of 'beauty' as to do something unmentionable to 'lovely pictures from Bermuda'? What kind of person plays the piano every night in the public rooms of a resort hotel that attracts a **convention** of advertising men? Certainly a person who actually drove into a tree or even threatened to drive into one would disrupt others' composure and attract attention to himself." This is a legitimate presentation of the "other side" of the case - that is, somewhat against - of the misfit hero, although French like most critics notes that his behavior is possibly unconscious or compulsive. Probably the fairest view, taken by many critics, is that the misfit hero is a person in conflict with himself, and is a combination of nice and unnice qualities. Wiegand suggests interestingly that these major **protagonists** have a spiritual illness, "banana fever," which renders them incapable of distinguishing between significant and insignificant experiences - incapable of mature judgment, in other words. Ihab Hassan, who has commented at length and aptly on Salinger, characterizes the internal conflict as one between the "assertive vulgarian" and the "responsive outsider." In any case this hero is usually isolated and is attempting to break out of his isolation, because like all humans he wants and needs warmth and love. Hassan makes an interesting point that the outsider sometimes reaches out by a "rare quixotic gesture" (that is, absurd but tender and meaningful - and unorthodox, unexpected), such as the wistfully recollected act of Walt, in "Uncle Wiggily in Connecticut," of placing his hand on Eloise's stomach, which is so beautiful, he says, that he ought to stick his other hand out of the train window, to be fair - in this instance, Eloise feels loved and cherished. (These gestures often embody what Salinger means by "nice," as discussed below.)How would most people react to being accused of staring at a nonexistent tattoo? How would people react to a man so disrespectful of age and femininity as to ask a grandmother about her plans for passing away? It is further remarked (by French, for example) that the misfit **protagonist** is often portrayed as imaginatively gifted but physically handicapped, which suggests why these people are driven in upon themselves. Instances are Ramona, with her myopic lenses, or the Laughing Man, who is a physical monstrosity and therefore an outcast from society. As French explains, "whether from bitter personal experience, an inferiority complex, delusions of grandeur, or simply observation of others, Salinger is aware that internal and external beauty do not always accompany each other and that, since the insensitive world often perceives only exteriors, handsome hollow men [like Stradlater] flourish while physically handicapped but imaginative children suffer and are driven deeper into themselves." To Arthur Mizener this withdrawal signifies their war against evil; Leslie Fiedler looks upon it as a temptation to madness.

PHONY AND NICE WORLDS

In any case, these characters are embattled against a world which often seems confusingly phony and nice at the same time. "Niceness" (aptly characterized by Hassan as the "rare quixotic gesture" at times) means to Holden, for example, a little boy singing to himself "If a body catch a body coming through the rye," or the good feeling of wearing the red hunting cap, or holding hands with Jane Gallagher in the movies. Boo Boo Tannenbaum is also "nice" in her awareness of what pleases a little boy-pickles, key chains, racing up the hill and winning against him mom-or what hurts that little boy-having daddy called a "kike", which he believes to be a thing with string flying in the sky. "Phoniness" is in fact "squalor" (which is what makes the story "For Esme-with Love and Squalor" such a perfect representation of Salinger's view of the world), whether in the ugliness of Eloise's life in Connecticut, or in Sergeant X's disillusioned and neurotic postwar universe, or in all the things Holden finds distasteful; although, as Warren French rightly points out, Salinger seems more "concerned with the effects rather than the causes of the human predicament" - that is, how to get along in a world of niceness and squalor. (Impressions of niceness and squalor in the world have also been viewed, as by French, from an internal angle, as "the manic and depressive extremes of Salinger's vision.") Some critics, though, see the tension between these extremes as "too much," beyond credibility, perversely ambiguous. Aldridge, for example, argues that Holden's world is a "compound of urban intelligence, juvenile contempt, and New Yorker sentimentalism," although French counters with the assertion that Aldridge has "no concept of the moral complexity of urban life." And Maxwell Geismar finds Salinger inconclusive, especially in *The Catcher in the Rye*, subscribing to "the New Yorker school of ambiguous finality."

CRUCIAL MOMENTS-EPIPHANIES-OF COMPASSION AND GROWTH OR REBIRTH

In most of Salinger's writings "love" is a crucial issue, and in the more optimistic ones it brings about growth or rebirth, although critics differ as to when this "salvation" has been accomplished. Of "The Laughing Man," for example, Hassan insists that the Chief's storytelling powers could not save him from a frustrating love experience, whereas Wiegand sees John Gedsudski as "sublimating" through art. Gwynn and Blotner perhaps restore the proper focus of this story by pointing out that it is the recollected experience of a mature man of a crucial or humanizing incident at age nine. Or take the suffering of little Lionel Tannenbaum-as Wiegand points out, the hypersensitive **protagonist** is sometimes comforted by a rare understanding parent such as Boo Boo Tannenbaum (who, to distort Hassan's phrase a bit, we might regard as one long extended "rare quixotic gesture" herself).

The efficacy of love is certainly the optimistic side of Salinger's works. Dan Wakefield comments in a way representative of many critics in saying that Salinger "speaks for all who have not lost hope-or even if they have lost hope, have not lost interest-in the search for love and morality in the present-day world." He stresses that, by taking the trouble to explore "love and squalor" in the modern world, Salinger is demanding that we re-examine ourselves and our values. The "hope" Salinger seems to hold out, then, is like Carl F. Strauch's (Wisconsin Studies in Contemporary Literature) theory about Holden, that he "psychologically dies only to be reborn into the world of Phoebe's innocence and love," which in turn starts his "own psychological regeneration." This is of course like Esme's gesture to Sergeant X, with a similar regeneration set in process. Or, as Warren French puts it, we have not only the story of Holden's nervous breakdown (which would be merely pessimistic) but "the story of the breaking down of Holden's self-centeredness and his gradual acceptance of the world that has rejected him."

It would appear then that Salinger's present-day appeal lies in his presentation of these misfit heroes in a world which can be quite destructive to the self yet occasionally offers a chance for growth-real maturing - and regeneration through love and compassion. As French suggests, Salinger is pleading for a world of values that "seem worth striving for," whether provided through a revised system of education or by other more personal means of genuine, more meaningful relationships between adults and children or adults and adults. In depicting both niceness and squalor, Salinger proves himself no "sentimentalizer," offering an easy assumption of either/or thinking and solutions. He asks not only that his children be helped to mature, but that, imperatively, his adults recognize certain phoniness and materialism, and in so doing, mature also. This is the note, perhaps, that his readers respond to. Ernest Jones, in writing about *The Catcher in the Rye*, has stated it excellently: the novel is "not at all something rich and strange, but what every sensitive 16-year-old since Rousseau has felt, and of course what each of us is certain he has felt." According to Jones, then, Salinger's appeal is that he provides "a case history of all of us."

THE CATCHER IN THE RYE

. . . .

THE IDEAS IN THE CATCHER IN THE RYE

Question: What is the **theme** of *The Catcher in the Rye*?

Answer: The **theme** of any work of art is arrived at by first deciding what the subject is. In *The Catcher in the Rye*, the subject is growing up. Now, the attitude that the author puts forth about his subject is what we call the **theme**. Therefore, the theme, in its broadest sense, would be the difficulty of growing up, the lonely and arduous voyage from innocence to experience.

Question: Is this **theme** in the mainstream of American literature?

Answer: Yes. Perhaps because our nation and traditions are so young, many prominent American novelists have used the **theme** of a young person's initiation to experience. The loneliness that Holden feels in his quest is also the reason that Ishmael in Melville's *Moby Dick* goes on the whaling voyage. The adventures and moral quest in Twain's *Huckleberry Finn* also parallel the continual search for order that Holden undertakes. Crane's *The Red Badge of Courage*, as well as other novels, shows the same preoccupation with psychological growth and moral awareness as does *The Catcher in the Rye*. The rebellion against genteel language and the subjective, individualistic way of telling the story also are very American. It is probable that in his use of colloquial language, Salinger was radically influenced by Ring Lardner.

Question: Should Holden be considered a typical or an unusual American youth?

Answer: Although Holden's sensitivity and intelligence are heightened for the purpose of dramatizing his character, he shares, to a considerable extent, the problems of all American youth.

Question: What are some of the chief difficulties that Holden faces as an adolescent?

Answer: Holden's main problems are honesty and egotism. Holden cannot really accept the death of his brother Allie. He idealizes him to the point where it interferes with his ability to make new friendships. He desires to be honest, which demands facing the problems of life, but he wants to protect all other children from having to face them. His sincerity leads him to lie, which beclouds his honesty, and forces him to wonder about his ability to be honest. This general pattern, i.e., a self-conscious examination of himself, leads him to doubt all his motivations, as when he dismisses the notion of being a lawyer. Holden feels that self-gratifying motives cannot be separated from any good intention. Holden, preoccupied with self, has a confused vision of the real objects in life. One of the evidences of Holden's growth is stated in the last chapter when Holden finally learns how to miss people.

Question: What does Holden's concern for the ducks symbolize?

Answer: Holden identifies with the innocent creatures and wants to know what fate has in store for them. It is symbolic of his desire to know about nature.

Question: What is the significance of Holden's relationship with his parents?

Answer: His relationship with his parents intensifies his general alienation because they do not seem to give him personal direction and warmth. He fails to see that their way of life can offer any solution for his problems.

Question: Does Holden change?

Answer: Yes. At the end of the book he does not desire to run away from home, and his concern for people has become more positive.

Question: Is the novel pessimistic or optimistic?

Answer: If one accepts Holden's growth of vision, then the novel must be considered optimistic. If, however, a reader feels that the growth does not counterbalance the painful struggle, the Holden's adolescence is both pessimistic and pathetic. The novel, of course, would be very pessimistic if Holden did not develop a new vision and purpose in life through his difficulties.

The answer also may vary according to whether the reader is afraid that Holden will be-or will not be-cured in the rest home.

Question: May a novel about an adolescent be significant to adults?

Answer: Yes. The universality of the **theme** cannot be overstated. If adult society cannot identify with the struggles of the young attempting to reach maturity, then adult society has no hope of maintaining a position of leadership. Without leadership, institutions would no longer give direction but merely propagandize. Social progress and communication is a two-way street which demands that the young understand the old and vice versa. Holden's growth in awareness and responsible acceptance is the most dramatic event in the book, but it must be matched by a mutual movement of comprehension on the part of adult society if it is to mean anything.

Question: What is Holden's attitude toward religion?

Answer: Holden satirizes the sermon by the wealthy undertaker. He sees the false image that is created in the connection between spirituality and material success. For the same reason he admires the charity of the nuns. He feels that they are directly committed to the principle of charity. Yet he pities them, even though they stand in direct contrast with the false, "ego" satisfying charity of some of his socialite neighbors, because they appear out of touch with reality.

Question: What is Holden's attitude toward sex?

Answer: Holden's sensitivity and normal teen-age pre-occupation with it can be seen throughout the novel. He is always talking of "flits" and he runs from Antolini's house in fear of being attacked.

Question: Is Holden a snob?

Answer: No. Holden is too genuinely concerned about people. In fact he is quite the opposite of a snob because he feels sorry for those who are not as privileged as he is. Although Holden's taste occasionally shows that he comes from a wealthy family, he does not express a feeling of superiority on the basis of wealth or social advantage.

THE FORM OF THE CATCHER IN THE RYE

Question: What is the over-all structural pattern of the novel?

Answer: The novel's shape is that of a circle. It begins in a California rest home, where Holden starts telling about the experiences which lead to his breakdown. The end of the novel returns to the rest home, completing the circle. Salinger intensifies and rounds out the circular structure of the novel by repeating the same symbols and **themes** at the conclusion of the novel that he used at the beginning.

Question: In what literary tradition can *The Catcher in the Rye* be placed?

Answer: *The Catcher in the Rye* is a novel about the development or maturation of the hero. There are many examples of this type in American and world literature, such as Twain's *The Adventures of Huckleberry Finn*, Crane's *The Red Badge of Courage*, Joyce's *A Portrait of the Artist as a Young Man*, Lawrence's *Sons and Lovers*, Faulkner's *The Bear,* and Mann's *The Magic Mountain.*

In a rapidly changing world this type of novel has a strong universal appeal.

Question: What effects come from Salinger's use of point of view?

Answer: *The Catcher in the Rye* is an example of subjective, first-person narrative. Everything we learn comes from and through Holden, who is the major character. The effect is not only to engage the reader directly in the novel but also to create depth. The reader must realize that Holden can only present things as a seventeen-year-old; it is up to the reader to evaluate Holden's personality and character through what he does choose to present. This places a burden on the reader to dig deeply into the meaning of things.

Question: What role does language play in the development of character and action in *The Catcher in the Rye*?

Answer: The colloquial and slang language serves to heighten the characterization of Holden Caulfield as well as control the pace of the novel. Holden's off-hand speech serves to demonstrate his inarticulate yet rebellious personality. He uses the same word in many different contexts, which forces the reader to pay close attention in order to appreciate the exact shades of meaning Holden intends.

Question: What are some of the more important symbols in the novel?

Answer: The three most important symbols are the song by Robert Burns, the red hunting hat, and the sports **imagery** which appears throughout. The title, which comes from a mishearing of the song, indicates Holden's great desire to have a transcendent moral purpose, to save children from any loss of innocence. Linked with the song title is the cap worn in reverse, which is the distinctive apparel of a baseball catcher. This inversion of the hunting cap, a symbol of man as the hunter, indicates that Salinger sees the hunting instinct in a different manner now. Man's struggle is elevated to the level of a moral quest. The red hat links Holden with the tradition of hunter, but Holden's passivity obviously makes him a new kind of hunter. Indeed, he is more the hunted than the hunter. The hunting hat is also linked to the general game and sport **imagery** in the novel. How you play the game, or whether you play the game, indicates your attitude to life. Holden, the reformer as well as the rebel, wants to make the rules more human, more acceptable to man.

Question: Is the structure of *The Catcher in the Rye* well a balanced?

Answer: Some critics have argued that the structure of the book falls apart when Holden does not follow through with his plan to run away. Phoebe, they argue, does not provide sufficient motivation for Holden's dramatic reversal. This criticism came quite early in the reception of the novel, and has since been well refuted. There are several reasons for Holden's reversal. Holden is very attached to his family; his tenderness for Phoebe and his memories of Allie are the most forceful relationships he has. Furthermore, Holden is running away from responsibility, not an unbearable family life. His struggle does not take the form of a direct clash between personalities. Holden's desire to escape his fraudulent environment is not without a sense of the loss of family that will accompany this separation. Therefore, when Holden decides not to leave because of his responsibility to Phoebe, this comes quite naturally to him. The motivation is subtle and complex just as the characterization of Holden is. The book is carefully and successfully well balanced.

Question: Is Holden an heroic figure?

Answer: Certainly Holden is not heroic in the traditional sense. Rather, he fits into the modern anti-heroic hero. He is not conventionally successful in his undertakings. Obviously Holden's strength does not rest in the traditional successes. Instead he is functioning on a different level, he is fighting a *Don Quixote* type of battle in order to restore moral order. Holden is heroic in the deepest sense because he truly battles against sham and corruption. His nobility does not reside in his external success but rather in his spiritual struggle.

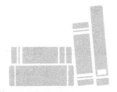

BIBLIOGRAPHY AND GUIDE TO
FURTHER RESEARCH

· ·

Aldridge, John L. "*The Society of Three Novels*," in *In Search of Heresy*. 1956, New York. Says reader of *The Catcher in the Rye* identifies with the **protagonist** but gains no insights; there is pathos without tragedy.

Belcher, William F. and James W. Lee, editors. J. D. *Salinger and the Critics*. 1962, Belmont paperback.

Bowen, Robert O. "The Salinger Syndrome: Charity against Whom?" *Ramparts*, I (May, 1962), 52–60.

Branch, Edgar. "Mark Twain and J. D. Salinger: A Study in Literary Continuity," *American Quarterly*, IX (Summer, 1957), 144–58.

Breit, Harvey. "Reader's Choice," *Atlantic*, CLXXXVIII (August, 1951), 82.

Carpenter, Frederic I. "Adolescent in American Fiction," *English Journal*, XLVI (September, 1957), 313–19.

Corbett, Edward P. J. "Raise High the Barriers, Censors," *America* (November 19, 1960), 441–43.

Costello, Donald P. "The Language of *The Catcher in the Rye*," *American Speech*, XXXIV (October, 1959), 172–81.

Davis, Tom. "J. D. Salinger: 'Some Crazy Cliff' Indeed," *Western Humanities Review*, XIV (Winter, 1960), 97–99. Catcher related to doctrines of Mahayana Buddhism, in which Salinger has shown interest.

Fiedler, Leslie. "The Eye of Innocence," in *No! In Thunder*. 1960, Boston. See also Love and Death in the American Novel, 1960, New York, discussion of Salinger and Jack Kerouac.

French, Warren. *J. D. Salinger* (Twayne Authors). 1963, New York. A comprehensive, scholarly yet interesting study.

Geismar, Maxwell. "J. D. Salinger: The Wise Child and the New Yorker School of Fiction," in *American Moderns: From Rebellion to Conformity*. 1958, New York.

Green, Martin. "Amis and Salinger: The Latitude of Private Conscience," *Chicago Review*, II (Winter, 1958), 20–25.

Gwynn, Frederick L. and Joseph L. Blotner. *The Fiction of J. D. Salinger*. 1958, Pittsburgh. A "monograph" on Salinger, the first. A brief and useful summary of author's achievements.

Grunwald, Henry Anatole, editor. *Salinger: A Critical and Personal Portrait*. 1962, New York. Interesting collection of about two dozen critical articles along with a lengthy introduction by editor.

Hansford, Martin. "The American Problem of Direct Address," *The Western Review*, XVI (Winter, 1952), 101–14.

Hassan, Ihab H. "Rare Quixotic Gesture: The Fiction of J. D. Salinger," in *Radical Innocence: Studies in the Contemporary Novel*. 1961. Princeton, N.J.

Havemann, Ernest. "The Search for the Mysterious J. D. Salinger," *Life*, Nov. 3, 1961, pp. 129–44. Recounts an unsuccessful visit to Cornish, N.Y., to interview Salinger.

Hermann, John. "J. D. Salinger: Hello Hello Hello," *College English*, XXII (January, 1961), 262–64. Discussion of Esme.

Hicks, Granville. "J. D. Salinger: Search for Wisdom," *Saturday Review*, XLII (July 25, 1959), 13–30.

Jacobs, Robert G. "J. D. Salinger's *The Catcher in the Rye*: Holden Caulfield's 'Goddam Autobiography,' *Iowa English Yearbook* (Fall, 1959), 9–14.

Jones, Ernest. "Case History of All of Us," *Nation*, CLXXIII (Sept. 1, 1951), 176.

Kaplan, Charles. "Holden and Huck: The Odysseys of Youth," *College English*, XVIII (November, 1956), 76–80.

Kazin, Alfred. "J. D. Salinger: 'Everybody's Favorite,'" *The Atlantic*, CCVIII (August, 1961), 27–31.

Kegel, Charles H. "Incommunicability in Salinger: *The Catcher in the Rye*," *Western Humanities Review*, XI (Spring, 1957), 188–90.

Laser, Marvin, and Norman Fruman, editors. *Studies in J. D. Salinger*. 1963, Los Angeles. Reviews and critical articles, emphasis on *Catcher*.

Levine, Paul. "J. D. Salinger: The Development of the Misfit Hero," *Twentieth Century Literature*, IV (October, 1958), 92–99.

Longstreth, T. Morris. "*Review of The Catcher in the Rye*," *The Christian Science Monitor* (July 19, 1951), 7.

Marks, Barry A. "Holden in the Rye," *College English*, XXIII (March, 1962), 507.

Marple, Anne. "Salinger's Oasis of Innocence," *New Republic*, CXLV (Sept. 18, 1961), 22–23.

Marsden, Malcolm M., editor. *If You Really Want to Know: A Catcher Casebook.* 1963, New York.

Martin, Dexter. "Holden in the Rye," *College English*, XXIII (March, 1962), 507–08.

McCarthy, Mary. "J. D. Salinger's Closed Circuit," *Harper's Magazine*, CCXXV (October, 1962), 46–47.

Mizener, Arthur. "The Love Song of J. D. Salinger," *Harper's Magazine*, CCXVIII (February, 1959), 83–90.

Salinger, J. D. *The Catcher in the Rye.* 1951, Boston (Bantam edition).

_____. *Nine Stories.* 1953, Boston (Signet edition).

_____. *Franny and Zooey.* 1961, Boston (Bantam edition).

Seng, Peter J. "The Fallen Idol: The Immature World of Holden Caulfield," *College English*, XXIII (December, 1961), 203–09.

Steiner, George. "The Salinger Industry," *Nation* (November 14, 1959), 360–63. His social criticism.

Updike, John. "Anxious Days for the Glass Family," *New York Times Book Review* (Sept. 17, 1961), 1, 52. Reviewed by a contemporary novelist and short story writer.

Wakefield, Dan. "Salinger and the Search for Love," *New World Writing* #14, New York, 1958.

Wells, Arvin R. "Huck Finn and Holden Caulfield: The Situation of the Hero,"
    The Ohio University Review, II.

Wiegand, William. "J. D. Salinger: Seventy-Eight Bananas," *Chicago*
    II (Winter, 1958), 3–19.

Wisconsin Studies in Contemporary Literature, III, No. 3 (Winter,
    A valuable Salinger issue.

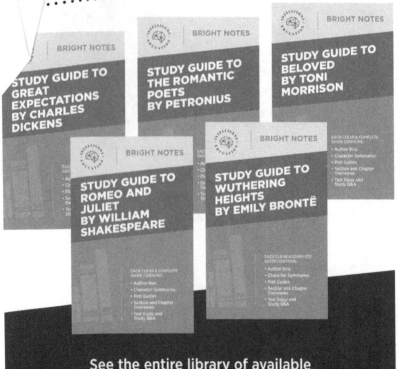